MAN UP

THE JOURNEY TO BECOMING A SON OF GOD

Brian E. Sherwood

ISBN 978-1-64349-186-8 (paperback)
ISBN 978-1-64349-188-2 (hardcover)
ISBN 978-1-64349-187-5 (digital)

Christian Faith Publishing, Inc.
832 Park Avenue
Meadville, PA 16335
www.christianfaithpublishing.com

Unless otherwise indicated, all Scripture quotations are taken from The Living Bible copyright © 1971. Used by permission of Tyndale House Publishers, Inc., Carol Stream, Illinois 60188. All rights reserved.

Printed in the United States of America

Dedicated to my mom… I loved our God talks.

The Three *W*s

Why am I writing this book? The Holy Spirit is leading me and flowing through me with the information to be placed in this book. I am just the vehicle for writing it down.
Who is the audience? All men, young, old, and in between.
What's the message? To let all men know that Christian men are not weak, and that God loves them and wants them to become the powerful and humble sons of God he created them to be.

> For all whom are led by the Spirit of God
> are Sons of God. (Rom. 8:14, TLB)

The Son of God became a man to enable men to become sons of God.

—C.S. Lewis

Contents

Preface

Dear Friend,

God wants you to *man up* and live the life you were meant to live; the life God created you to live, the powerful humble life as a son of God.

In the Bible scripture John 3:16, it says, "For God so loved the world so much that he gave his only son so that anyone whom believes in him shall not perish but have eternal life."

I firmly believe that it would be dishonoring to God not to live up to what he created us to be. Could you imagine giving up your son to die for the world so that it would be a better place, then having the world not live up to what it could be? I don't know about you, but I would be completely devastated.

I am extremely honored and blessed to God for leading you to pick up this book. I encourage you to thumb through it and begin to read it. My belief is that as you read, you will be filled with the Heavenly Father and his love for you.

Trials Turn into Testimonies

Also, I believe you cannot fully teach what you have not experienced. As the Holy Spirit is flowing through me to write this book of my journey to becoming a son of God, I will share the people that God has put into my life during this journey and experiences that I have gone through.

What I have gone through in God's boot camp and "advance individual training" or AIT has helped me to understand that I needed God the Heavenly Father and will always need him to lead me, guide me, train me, I needed to reach out to him, asking him to please guide me, teach me, to become strong in my need to as I minister to other men whom will be going through the same or similar situations/experiences.

As I have learned of the years is to have great relationships is like taking care of flowers or a garden. They need to be watered, fed, and nurtured continually to make them grow into what they are meant to be. The same goes for my relationship with the Heavenly Father, Lord Jesus, and the Holy Spirit, I need to dwell in them continually to enhance my relationship with them.

All praise, glory, and honor go to God, without whom I am nothing

Introduction

I believe today, in the year of 2017, that the world is in a state of chaos. And I also believe the enemy, Satan, has caused this chaos, it is the enemy's focus to steal, kill, and destroy everything good.

What the world is in a need of now more than ever is men filled with Christ to lead and guide (be a shepherd) to themselves, their families, their employment, their place of living, and their country. To be strong men; men of great character; Spirit-filled men.

I hope that if you have not accepted Christ into your life that after reading this book that you will accept Christ. And if you have already accepted Christ into your life but may have been ignoring his calling for your life that you will fulfill that calling.

Jesus is a builder of men—men of great courage call unto him to build you into the powerful/humble man he wants you to be.

1

I Am Weak, Are You?

Each time he said, "No, But I am with you; that is all you need. My power shows up best in weak people," Now I am glad to boast about how weak I am, I am glad to be a living demonstration of Christ's power, instead of showing off my own power and abilities. Since I know it is all for Christ's good, I am quite happy about "the thorn" and about insults and hardships, persecutions and difficulties for when I am weak, then I am strong—the less I have, the more I depend upon him. (2 Cor. 12:9–10, TLB)

But how is it that Christian men are viewed to be weak in today's society/culture? I know for myself I had that view for many, many years. Until I entered God's boot camp for me. I had no idea just how wrong I was.

A little about me: I grew up in a male-leaderless home. It was not because there was not a male authority figure in the home. My parents were divorced when I was quite young, around five years old. My mom remarried and two years later, we moved several hundred miles from where my dad lived. My stepfather, I believe, did the best he could from the teaching that he had. At the time, I always wondered if he did not like me or was it he just ignored me. The male leadership that I received growing up was *not* Christ-centered to help me become the man God wanted me to be.

I lived in a small logging town in the Pacific northwest until I graduated high school, where a "strong" man worked out in the woods. He worked hard and played even harder, drinking beer and fighting other men, especially when even slightly challenged. Going to church and/or even mentioning God was a sign of weakness.

Growing up, I did not attend church much only when my mom and stepdad must have been searching for their something, for their own journey did we go to church, and most of the time, we had to be told that if we did not go, we could not ride our motorcycles. This was during third grade, fourth grade, and fifth grade years. I don't remember much about the pastor/minister. In fact I did not attend church again until I met my first wife, who grew up Catholic. I was twenty-three then in my viewpoint was the priests in the Catholic Church and viewed that you only got God when you were in church not that knowing he could/would be with me all time and I could have a close personal relationship with him.

✠

As a young boy, growing up strong meant you played competitive sports (peewees, pop warner, junior high, high school); you stood up to all challengers; you did not back down; or turn your back and walk away. If you did, you would get called many names (chicken, weenie, coward, etc.) or possibly called out to fight. And if you did not fight, it got even worse verbally.

For me, football, basketball, baseball, any type of automobile, motorcycle, and boat racing were interests of mine.

In sports, if you played against any Christian school, the game usually was a very lopsided score. It was viewed that the Christian school boys were "less than." Even as I got older, playing softball in men's leagues the worst member on the team would be considered the most coveted player on any church league team (physically strong). Growing up, I never thought of having mental, emotional, or spiritual strength, just physical strength.

As I got older, I continued to search for information on what it meant to be a male leader. I would soak up information from other males whom I considered were good men. I would not ask questions; I would observe, soak in what I felt was important, more so how to do things, build things, fix things. Looking back, I never heard or received any information about life.

If I asked questions growing up, most of the time, they were met with some sort of verbal insult, "How come you don't know, you dummy?" Or "I already told you once. I am not explaining it again." "What do I have to do, draw you a picture?" (Later in life I did become aware that I learned and understood best following a picture for instructions was more effective than printed/spoken/written words).

Living in a logging town, I easily identified with blue-collar workers. Then in my thirties, I moved into the white-collar world. later with work assignments of business executives, and I did not get my higher education degrees until I was in my mid-forties.

I have been married twice and divorced twice; the root of the problem in these marriages as well as relationships in between and after is *me*. I was not a leader in the relationship. I was not strong, my confidence covered up my insecurities of not feeling good enough, feeling lost. I did not know at the time what the following scripture in the Bible meant:

> After he and his wife are united so
> that they are no longer two, but one.
> (Mk 10:8, TLB)

How I was treating my partner was in fact how I was treating myself. I wanted to avoid conflict because of my need to be liked and loved. During my divorce and after we divorced, I did not attend church. I was just floating around like a lost sheep, looking for my shepherd. As I started traveling more for my work, the Lord brought those pastors who were on TV into my purview as I would channel surf in the morning before going to work. Or in the evening after work, Joyce Meyer, Joel Osteen, Joseph Prince were the three I would continue to find.

✝

I had no strong foundation to build my life on. I was doing my best to "fake it" until "I make it," trying, searching, reading every self-help book that I could get my hands on. Attending many, many classes, seminars trying to learn life, business, spirituality, and love. Which were all good to get me to where I am today. However, I believe the road/journey to God would have been shorter if I would have listen to/been aware of God talking to me, reaching out wanting to show me the way, his way to have the strong foundation "The Rock" in which I could build upon.

> All who listen to my instructions and fol-
> low them are wise, like a man who builds
> his house on solid rock. (Matt. 7:24)

So in my first talks with God, I was timid and awaiting the verbal abuse that I used to receive as child growing up; however, it never came. All that came was unconditional love, support, and guidance from my Heavenly Father.

I am proud to proclaim that I am weak; I cannot do this life by myself and live to what God wants me to be. To be at my strongest, I need God every minute of every day.

My beliefs about Christian men being weak have been "shattered" from what I have learned and experienced the last several years. We are at our strongest when we are with God.

2

Bread Crumbs

As I continued my journey through life, God knew that I was looking for him, wanting to come to him, but I did not know how to get there, to get home, so he put out bread crumbs for me to follow and get me home to him, and hopefully not get lost along the way.

I believe God brings his message for each of us individually through our interests and likes for us to see that is he everywhere and wants us to find him. For me who grew up in a very small town, who played sports and grew into a business executive, he laid down the breadcrumbs for me to follow.

There have been many crumbs for me. However, these are some that have stood out to me:

Christian music
Coach Joe Gibbs—*Game Plan for Life*
Joyce Meyer
Joel Osteen
Joseph Prince

Lonnie Berger—*Every Man a Warrior*
The Robertsons: *Duck Dynasty Reality Show*
Titan—The Life of John D. Rockefeller Sr. by Ron Chernow
UWMC—my physician

Christian Music

Music has been one of the biggest factors that has touched my life over the years, listening to various stations as kid while at my grandparents, the song that was playing at the prom during that slow dance or that special time I had with my girlfriend/wife...

God has used Christian music as one of the ways he has talked to me, especially when I was at my bottom and could not find a way back out of the valley of despair. He used music of artists such as Mercy Me, Danny Gokey, Hillary Scott, Hillsong, Jeremy Camp, Chris Tomlin, Crowder Phillips, Craig & Dean, and many others and used it a bread crumb for me to continue my journey to him and to feel all the love that he has for me.

> Remember what Christ taught and let his words enrich your lives and make you wise; teach them to each other and sing them out in psalms and hymns and spiritual songs, singing to the Lord with thankful hearts. (Col. 3:16, TLB)

✝

Coach Gibbs—Game Plan for Life

Coach Gibbs is and was involved in several interests that I could relate to racing and football. He used analogies in his books that I could understand and relate them to my life.

His books, *Game Plan for Life* and *Game Plan for Life Chalk Talks Devotional* God used them as a bread crumb for me to continue to have faith and look to him as the head coach of my life.

The following are several areas that touched me and help me in my walk with God.

The perfect coach. Growing up, I played various sports. I always had a coach that would help me become the best I could become. Some were good and became mentors of mine; others not as good. However, there was always a coach. As I got older, I thought having a coach was a sign of weakness. I should be able to do this as I am an adult. Again, that is where I was not able to perform at my best. I was not winning at life, I was not getting blown out 60 – 0. However, I was behind by several touchdowns.

Coach explained in his book that in the game of life, God—our head coach—is the single most important factor in winning in life…

The Perfect Game Plan

> For I know the plans I have for you. Declares the Lord. "Plans to prosper you and not to harm you, plans to give you hope and a future. (Jer. 29:11, TLB)

Coach writes that on Wednesdays, when he was coaching, he would give each player his playbook for the next game. Then they would practice the plays—defenses and strategies for the rest of the week. And as a coach, he wanted his players to have the best possible advantage that would increases the chances for a win.

He continues to say this is what he believes God does for us. As our head coach for life in which God wants us to win the biggest game of all. He has done that in His Word, the Bible. But are we diligently studying it?

Learning from Financial Disaster

I was pleasantly surprised at the honesty that came out of Coach Gibbs. He had made a bad choice that made him responsible for paying off a lot of money on a bad investment. I also had made some bad decisions about money and felt that there was no way out from the weight that put me under.

Coach said, "There were more miraculous events that came out of this calamity, but the biggest lesson I learned that I needed to understand Gods plan for my money. His Biblical principles of stewardship."

Wisdom for Dealing with Life Challenges

Coach wrote in his book that he when he deals with life challenges, he says the following to God.

"I am done, I'm turning this over to you, you know what I want to do in life, but I cannot do this. I am just going to have to trust you."

I had to do my best and let God handle the rest.

Trusting the Playbook

In coach's prayer at the end of the chapter named "Trusting the Playbook":

> Father, thank you for giving me the Bible as the playbook for my life… within its pages are the answers to the challenges I face. He me to understand and come to rely on the Bible daily. I want to live my life to the fullest and know You better. Please give me the patience and help me find the right tools to make the Bible my playbook for living and winning the most important game of all—the game of life, amen.

Joyce Meyer, Joel Osteen, Joseph Prince

During the years that I was traveling for business, living out of a suitcase, staying in hotels, there was always those times in which I couldn't sleep, usually in middle of the night.

So, I would be channeling surfing to see what was on television and almost 95 percent of the time I would come upon either a Joyce Meyer, Joel Osteen, or Joseph Prince thirty-minute television spot. And always, and I do mean

✝

always, I would hear something that God wanted me to hear.

There was a stretch of time in which I would wake up consistently at the times of these shows, and I would just laugh and turn the TV on and go to the channel in which the show was on and say, "Okay, God, what am I to learn today?"

Jesus was planting seeds to grow within me. Just exactly like in his parable of the sower as written in Matthew 13:1–8, and I am extremely thankful that my soil was good enough that the seeds are now producing the crops he wants from me.

> A farmer was sowing grain in his fields. As he scattered the seed across the ground, some fell beside the path, and the birds came and ate it. And some fell on rocky soil where there was little depth of earth, the plants sprung up quickly enough in the shallow soil, but the hot sun soon scorched them, and they withered and die, for they had little root. Other seeds fell among thorns, and the thorns choked out the tender blades. But some fell on good soil, and produced a crop that was thirty, sixty, and even a hundred times as much as he had planted. (Matt. 13:1–8, TLB)

✝

Lonnie Berger—Every Man a Warrior

I was introduced to Lonnie Berger's book series *Every Man a Warrior* shortly after my being let go from my job that I was working in Canada.

Every Man a Warrior is a discipleship course series designed to help men succeed in life. It is for men who want to become the warriors God intends. Equipping men in the areas where men fight and need to win.

At the start of the book, Lonnie said something that really got my attention. He said, "As Christian men we are constantly engaged in a war, whether we realize it or not, our life is the battle field and Satan our enemy."

I thought to myself, *Really, how could this be true?* However, in my learning in boot camp, I found that the enemy Satan wants to steal, kill, and destroy in all aspects of our lives from marriage and relationships, raising our children, managing money, our jobs, and career paths, staying morally pure, and making our lives count. These are the battlefields that enemy wages his war against us on, and if we are not trained and equipped with the skills necessary to fight and end well, most of us will lose. God wants to give you those skills to fight, win and end your life well.

> Be careful—watch out for attacks from Satan, your greatest enemy. He prowls around like a hungry, roaring lion, looking for someone to tear apart. (1 Pet. 5:8, TLB)

✝

The Robertsons: Duck Dynasty Books and Reality Show

The Robertson family, A family that I could easily relate to growing up in a small logging town in the Pacific northwest where there were lots of "good ole boys."

Not only did I watch the show, but I read most of their books, searching for the nuggets of information that God wanted me to receive.

This is one of the first times that I realized that I could be myself, talk about God, and how important he was in my life.

To me, the Robertson family was down-to-earth, humble, and happy, happy, happy.

> And now a word to you parents. Don't keep nagging your children, making them angry and resentful. Rather, bring them up with the loving discipline the Lord himself approves, with suggestions and godly advice. (Eph. 6:4, TLB)

Titan—The Life of John D. Rockefeller by Ron Chernow

God led me to read this book by Ron Chernow shortly after I moved to my dad's and I was at my lowest point. I felt I had lost everything and that there was no way that I was going to be abundant again.

During my prior work experience I did not know any successful Christian businessmen. This book shared with me Rockefeller's thought process on business and his belief in God.

Early in life, Rockefeller learned that God wanted his flock to earn money and donate or tithe back to him in a never-ending process. (Tithing is used to build the kingdom of God on the earth: to build churches, temples, missions, printed materials, etc. Other voluntary donations are also given to help the poor, those in need, missionaries, disaster relief victims, etc.)

Rockefeller believed it was a religious duty to get all he could honorably, and to give away all that he could. He said he was taught that way by a minister when he was young. His religious upbringing as a Baptist did not prohibit the accumulation of wealth, but did oppose its vain, ostentatious display.

Rockefeller had a humble desire to serve God, led prayer meetings, and he regarded God as an honorary shareholder of Standard Oil who had richly blessed his fortunes.

Once during a meeting with the press Rockefeller made this outburst to a reporter:

I believe the power to make money is a gift from God— just as are the instincts for art, music, literature, the doctors talent, the nurses, yours—to be developed and used to the best of our ability for the good of mankind. Having been endowed with the skills I possess, I believe it is my duty to make money and still more money, and to use the money I make for the good of my fellow man according to the dictates of my conscience.

✝

For Rockefeller believed there was a perfect fusion of Christianity and capitalism, I also took away from this book is that Rockefeller did not put other idols in front of his relationship with God. Running Standard Oil, making money was always secondary to his commitment to God.

Rockefeller loved to indulge in his two consuming past times: God and golf.

> You must not have no idols; you must never worship carved images, obelisks or shaped stones for I am the Lord your God. (Lev. 26:1, TLB)

University of Washington Medical Center—My Physician

God sent me an angel in my general physician who practiced at the University of Washington Medical Center. In 2009, when I hit one of my biggest bottoms, he took extraordinary time with me. I went into have physical after my bad judgment took me out of my job, and my doctor took one look at me and told me I looked horrible and asked me what was going on.

I told him all that went on, and he said to that I needed to go through what I was going through with class and dignity; my main focus was for me to show my children that even though their father had hit bottom, I could pull myself out of it and do it with class. He then said he wanted to see me in thirty days for a follow-up.

I came back thirty days later, (I asked God to send sign every day to know that I was going to be ok which he did) he came in the exam room and said that I looked much better and asked what had been going on the last thirty days in which I told him. After he listened to me, he asked me if I liked football; I said yes. He said, "Let me give you a football analogy, he told me it was now half time of my life and I was in the locker room, and that I was losing the game, it was not like I was getting blown out 60-0, but I was down by a couple of touch downs and that I need to adjust my game plan and review how was I going to play in the second half of my life, and end up on the winning side of the score when I am called to go to heaven."

Two months had passed after that conversation, and I called the doctor's office and asked for an appointment with him. The receptionist stated that he was no longer practicing there, and they did not know where he was practicing at.

To this day, I do not know where he is at; however, I thank God for him placing this angel in my life and helping me when I needed it.

The truth is that as hard as it was for me during this time for me, I knew in my heart—even in the painful moment of half time of my life, that my God always gives me things that are best for me. This is the same God whom gave his only son to die on the cross for my sins. His plans for us are so much better than one we could ever make ourselves.

> For I know the plans I have for you, says the
> Lord, they are for good and for evil, to give
> you a future and a hope. (Jer. 29:11, TLB)

✝

3

God Finally Got My Attention

Over the years, God has tried to get my attention through putting various people/and or events in my life. He would try gently to get my attention, but I was not listening. I was not paying attention. Maybe I was just plain afraid to give up control and/or change how I was doing in life, to admit my way was not working. Whatever it was, I just plain would not hear him.

The analogy I like to use for myself (having a thick head) is that God had tried to get my attention by hitting me over the head with a piece of 2 × 4 piece of wood. That did not work. I went on with life (my free will, the one God gives all of us).

The form of the 2 × 4 was that over a seven-year period, I had been divorced (after twelve years of marriage), remarried, and divorced again.

Then he would try to get my attention using a 4 × 4 piece of wood, that would slow me down for a while. However, with my strong free will, not wanting to ask for help or wanting to change, I would continue to move forward in my life. The 4 × 4 came in the form of losing a job I had with a company for over twenty years. Secure in my job, making very good money, the loss was the result of self-inflicted ego-driven actions, thinking that the rules did not apply to me. The foreclosure on a house that I bought at the height of the housing market to flip, pull myself out of my financial rut. During this time, I was hurting, hurting really bad. I was thinking about suicide as I was driving back to my house (that would I give back to the bank), after my doctor's appointment (where I was told that I looked horrible and that I need to go through this issue with class), and from seeing two of my children on my Wednesday to be with them. I saw a semi-truck coming from the opposite way, and I said to myself, "I am done, I hurt so bad, I cannot go on." I went to drive in the oncoming traffic, but my steering wheel would not turn. I believe that my guardian angels where hanging on some kind of tight to not let the steering wheel turn into oncoming traffic. After that I went back to the house I would eventually lose, I lay on the living room floor for two days in the fetal position, just crying. I at this point in my life, I believed in God but did not have a relationship with him. Eventually, I would get up and I shouted out to God, "I cannot do this, I am hurting, I need a sign from you every day, every day to keep me going."

And as it says in Matthew 7:7–8, "Ask and you will find. Knock, and the door will be opened. For everyone who asks, receives, anyone who seeks, finds. If you only knock the door will be open."

For the next two months, every day, the Heavenly Father, the Lord Jesus, and the Holy Spirit sent me a sign

✝

that kept me going (the amount of time I needed for this to get my feet under me and begin to walk on my own). Even with the amount of pain that I went through my free will, my ego believed that I did not need any help; I did not need to follow the Heavenly Father.

Then God hit me over the head with a 6 × 6 piece of wood and finally knocked me to my knees, and then and only then while I was down on my knees, I asked God, "Please help me, I cannot go on any longer like this." I was broken; broken to the core of my very being, then and only then was I open and willing to let God totally in my life and guide me.

That 6 × 6 came over a two-year period in the form of

1. A loss of an executive position with a company in which I was making good money.
2. The loss of a relationship with a very amazing, beautiful, loving woman that I was in a relationship with for over five-and-a-half years. The stress of me not having meaningful employment to pay the bills for over eighteen months put our relationship over the edge. She did what God wanted her to do: she let me go, God wanted me to be by myself where I was not medicating with a good, well-paying job or a relationship with a woman. She was such a gift to me, and I am blessed, so grateful, and thank God for the time we spent together.
3. My two oldest daughters telling me how I ruined their lives and pulling away from me with no communications.

God placed two men in my life during this time frame of loss who have helped me tremendously along my journey. The first gentleman he brought to me came a couple of months before the loss of the executive position. I hired a gentleman for a position I had open. Little did I know at that time that he would turn out to be very instrumental for me in my walk with Christ. The second gentleman was recommended to me by a coworker at the Home Improvement Retail Store I was working at part-time to use as a counselor for the issues that I was going through.

Both men truly loved the Lord, loved talking about all the goodness that God brings the world, and I would come to find out over time that these men were sons of God. I will use Watchman as the name for the first gentleman, and Reverend for the second gentleman as I describe my time with them.

Before I was let go from my job as an executive director, the Watchman and I would have long talks about God, the Bible, the Commandments—especially the first and second commandments:

1. I am the Lord your god whom brought you out of Egypt, out of the land of slavery. You shall have no other Gods before me.
2. You shall not make for yourself an image in the form of anything in heaven above or on the earth beneath or in the waters below. You shall not bow down to them or worship them; for I, the LORD YOUR GOD, AM A JEALOUS GOD, PUNISHING THE CHILDREN FOR THE SIN OF THE PARENTS TO

THE THIRD AND FOURTH GENERATION OF THOSE
WHO HATE ME, but showing love to a thousand
generations of those who love me and keep my
commandments,

The Watchman asked me if I wanted to give my life to the Lord, I said yes. So, he took some olive oil placed it on my head and he me say the following:

"God, I believe that Jesus died on the cross for my sins. Please forgive me for all my sins. Jesus, I ask you to be my Lord and Savior. God, I now take you as my Father. Amen."

For the next fifteen months, I would be in almost daily contact with the Watchman, as I was reading the Bible, questions would come up and we would talk about them. I was thinking and believing now that I have asked God into my life for help he would "immediately" fix me, heal me so I will not suffer any longer, and now life will be so good. However, I was still having problems in my relationships with my girlfriend, my children, my ex-wife, etc.

But what I failed to understand is that this is a process, and that this process would take some time. Christianity is not a sprint, but it is a marathon.

Jesus did not just walk up and grab men (Simon (who was called "Peter"); Andrew, James, John, Philip, Bartholomew, Thomas, Matthew, Judas, Simon, Thaddeus, and James) and say, "Now you are now my disciples, I am making you sons of God, I have just given you all the information how you can do all of this." No! He trained them how, took them through his process; a training process aka boot camp. Like going through school. You start out in kindergarten, then to first grade, second, third… etc. Then you graduate high school; next level of higher education is say college or trade school. You are learning constantly, moving from one grade to the next. There were many who wanted to follow Jesus. At one time, there were seventy-two who were being trained, sent out on short-term missions or internships, but only twelve initially graduated and became the primary disciples of Christ.

We also talked about how the enemy, Satan's, purpose is the following as described scripture:

> The thief's purpose is to steal, kill, and destroy. (John 10:10, TLB)

Satan, the enemy, the thief, will use any means possible to come between the relationship of God and yourself. He will come in and cause a disturbance between your girl-friend/wife, your children, things going on at work, and yourself. Those things you most love, need, or want.

He will steal your joy; he will come into the body as a disease, cancer, etc.

The Watchman told me that God has given you and I armor in which we are to wear during this time of spiritual warfare:

> Last of all I want to remind your that your strength must come from the Lord's mighty power within you. Put on all of God's armor so that you will be able to

stand safe against all strategies and tricks of Satan.

For we are not fighting against people made of flesh and blood but of persons with that bodies—the evil rulers of the unseen world those mighty satanic beings and great evil princes of darkness who rule this world and against huge numbers of wicked spirits in the spirit world. So use every piece of God's armor to resist the enemy whenever he attacks, and when it is all over you will be standing up.

But to do this, you will need the strong belt of truth and the breastplate of God's approval. Wear shoes that are able to speed you on as you preach the Good News of peace with God.

In every battle you will need faith as you shield the fiery arrows aimed at you by Satan.

And you will need the helmet of salvation and the sword of the spirit which is the word of God.

Pray all the time, ask God for anything in line with the Holy Spirit's wishes. Plead with him, reminding him of your needs, and keep praying earnestly for all Christians everywhere. (Eph. 6:10–18, TLB)

I am here to tell you that when you come to accept Christ and start your relationship with him, the battle is on. During this process of your walk with God, you will need to rely on him more and more and you will become stronger and stronger, becoming a strong man in the Lord, not a weak man.

Much like going to a gym and building up your muscles, to be a physically strong man: you will need to consistently exercise, weightlifting, push-ups, sit-ups, pull-ups, etc. constantly to get stronger and stronger. Some mornings you may get up after a real hard exercising the day before sore and slow to move, but after a short period of time (at least for me), it feels awesome to know that I am getting stronger.

This is the same way in your walk with the Lord. You need to be consistent in your prayer and meditation, consistent in your reading of the Bible. Train in God's gym, my brother, become spiritually strong.

As I continued on my journey walking with God, my life was unraveling, a coworker at the Home Improvement Store asked me how things were going, and boy, howdy, that was all it took for me to let loose all that was going on in my life. After I got through explaining myself, they said, "I have someone for you to call that I think can help you." And they handed me the business card of the Reverend.

So that early evening in March, just after I received the business card with his number, I called the Reverend, explaining my situation of what was happening in my life, and that started my journey with the Reverend. Little did I know the Reverend would be such a huge influence on me.

✝

Later, I would realize that as I worked with the Reverend that he also was a Son of God, and as God worked through him to teach me.

We talked every day. Sometimes two or more times a day. He would always meet me where I was (emotionally/spiritually) at every situation.

The Reverend had been in the military as a minister in the Special Forces Rangers. He explained how training was in boot camp, and once graduated, how there was Advance Individual Training or AIT that each soldier received to help them with their specific area of specialty. The reverend was able to put what I was going through into scenarios in which I understood.

As I continued my journey with the Reverend, I started to feel that I really am a divine branch of God, and as a branch, I get all my nourishment from the tree of life, which is God.

My new mantra during this time was that God is leading me on a miraculous journey on which miracle after miracle will give way to miracle.

As I continued to focus on God's will for me and working on my faith that everything will work out, I would tell myself that all that I am is from God and to God. The gifts I hold his, not mine; they are to use as he chooses

After about three months, during one of my conversations with the Reverend, we had been talking about doing what God wanted us to do—I said that I was not sure what God had in mind for me to do. The Reverend said, "Let's pray about it for the next couple of weeks and when we get together again, we will share what has come to us." The time came for our next fellowship, and I still was really unsure of what God wanted from me. I knew that I wanted to get back into business, run companies, turnaround companies, something that I feel I was really good at. The Reverend let me know what God wanted me to do, which was to be a pastor of my own flock, (God would later tell me that I am to minister to men to become to become the powerful, humble men God created them to be.)

When I first heard this that I was to have my own flock—at first, I was a little taken aback, how much would I have to change—especially my personality—does God want me to change?

So, when the Reverend and I met the next time, I told him I was struggling with what God wanted me to do as I was unsure what to do and where to go next.

He gave me an analogy to think about. He asked me how many grocery stores there were in the town in which I lived. I said there were about four to six plus the little convenience stores.

He then asked if they were all the same. I said no.

He then asked me if I shopped at every one of these stores? And I said no. There were some I liked and some I did not care for.

He laughed and said yes, each one of the stores is unique and drew their own clientele.

He said just as pastors/ministers, each one is different and each one drew their own clientele or flock.

He said that God did not want me to change my personality; that he loved me for who I am, that God would draw the people whom were meant to shop at my store.

Now that I was able to understand that analogy I was able to accept fully what God wanted me to do.

So, I decided to make a contract with God.

Dated May 25, 2015

Dear God,
Back in December 2013, I told you what I wanted.

- Peace and calm in my life
- Solvency/financial freedom
- Positive cash flow
- Debt free
- Pay my bills on time
- Relationship with my girlfriend that is positive, healthy, loving, honest, and nurturing
- Right livelihood that feeds my soul positively and supplies my needs
- To be healthy physically, mentally, emotionally, and spiritually
- I want to be totally honest in all my communications with my girl-friend, my children, myself, and with everyone I speak to.

You talked to me/came to me right after that saying that you would make me more abundant than ever before, getting rid of

✝

my debt, give me what I asked for. You said that I would run/own my own business, helping people through your work/word through that business.

You also said that you would take it all away again if I turned my back on you.

I believed you and took your word for this.

Since that time, eighteen months ago I have been in a spiritual boot camp to be a soldier for you.

I was laid off from my job in Canada and have been unemployed and underemployed since then.

I have dealt with my ex-wife and the money and the children.

My relationship with xxxx has been strainful at best.

On a positive note, I have been closer to you than ever before. I asked you to mold me into the man you want me to be. Be the man of the house.

I have been blessed and grateful to you as you have provided me with two wonderful teachers.

- Brother the "Watchman"
- Brother the "Reverend"

The Watchman guided and taught me for over a year.

Now for the past two months, the Reverend has been my coach/mentor/teacher.

During this time with the Reverend he has spoke to me your words, to teach me, how to be the man of the house, how to be a better man in relationship with a woman.

The Reverend has also told me of two things you want me to do.

1. Is to move back into the house that I share with my girlfriend as a roommate to start off with and be the rock for her, to learn the lessons that I am to learn.

   Lord, I am willing to do this, and I ask you to continue to give me the signs that you are working in this with me.

2. The second item in your communication to the Reverend is that of my calling to do your work is that of a minister/pastor of my own flock. And that I would know this to be true as three people whom I don't know would come up to me

and tell me that you want me to become a minister.

Lord, I am willing to do what you have asked. However, I have several requests of you to ensure that you are with me and want me to do this as we go through this together.

1. Have three people unknown to me to tell me that you want me to be a pastor/minister.
2. Lord, I want to work directly for you, not any other religion organization but directly through to you.
3. To be able to do this full time I need your help to get rid of all my debt, become solvent/financially free and provide a steady income so that I can focus on the task at hand.
4. I need to work until my youngest children are graduated from high school which is in seven more years. Then I can be full time.
5. I want a wife/life partner that is fully vested in you, believes in you, will pray with me, and support me doing this work.

✝

6. I want to be an active pastor/minister while I am at the gym, riding my Harley, on the golf course. Continually to do the things I love, and thus, doing your work. I know that as I evolve with my free will, I may choose to pursue other interests, and I will pursue them with passion and with you by my side as I perform them.

7. I don't want to pay for Bible college, I will need you to ensure this gets done.

8. Help men, many men, be warriors, tough men of God.

Lord, this is my contract to you. This day May 25, 2015.

Brian Sherwood.

I was thinking and believing now that I have asked God into my life for help, he would "immediately" fix me, heal me not to suffer any longer. That now life will be so good. But what I failed to understand is that this is a process, and that this process would take some time.

As he was starting out on a trip, a man come running to him and knelt down and asked, "Good Teacher, what must I do to get into heaven?"

"Why do you call me good?" Jesus asked. "Only God is truly good!

"But as for your question—you know the commandments: don't kill, don't commit adultery, don't steal, don't lie, don't cheat, respect your mother and father."

"Teacher," the man replied, "I've never once broken a single one of those laws."

Jesus felt genuine love for this man as he looked at him. You lack only one thing, he told him, "Go and sell all you have and give the money to the poor—and you shall have treasure in heaven—and come, follow me."

Then the man's face fell, and he went sadly away, for he was very rich.

Jesus watched him go, then turned around and said to his disciples. It is *almost* impossible for the rich to get into the kingdom of God.

This amazed them, so Jesus said it again, "Dear children, how hard is it for those whom *trust* in riches to get into the kingdom of God!"

The disciples were incredulous! "Then who in the world can be saved, if not a rich man," they asked

✠

Jesus looked at them intently, then said, "Without God, it is utterly impossible! But with God everything is possible. (Mk 10:17–27, TLB)

God asked me nicely to follow him and commit to him. He would gently nudge me (2 × 4), then a little more aggressively (4 × 4), and finally he got my attention (with a 6 × 6).

Brothers, I am here to tell you that my experience that my process has not been easy whatsoever. However it has been so worth the grind.

As it states in the following Bible scripture:

And Jesus said; "Let me assure you that no one has ever given up anything—home, brothers, sisters, mother, father, children, or property—for the love of me and to tell others the Good News… Who won't be given back, a hundred times over, homes, brothers, sisters, mothers, children and land— with persecutions. (Mk 10:29–30, TLB)

4

You Are Not the Only One

In Lonnie Berger's *Every Man a Warrior* book, he states, "If you are going to bring men to maturity, they must be challenged. You don't build character and leadership skills by watering down the requirements, you don't send men to war without rigorous training, specific skills and expect them to win."

As I first was going through my "spiritual boot camp" I thought to myself, *Really, am I the only one going through this?* Then as I continued my journey, I became aware of the many men that have gone through their own boot camp, and here are a couple of biblical men that have gone through their boot camp.

Moses

(As described by Joseph Prince in one of this blogs)

> 1st 40 years of life for Moses was as an Egyptian prince, he became a mighty prince and orator.

Acts 7:22 However, God could not use him to deliver his people out of Egypt. The next 40 years of his life, Moses killed an Egyptian man and he fled Egypt and became a Shepherd and was no longer considered a mighty prince or an or an orator in fact Moses was now stuttering.

Exodus: 4:10 I am not a good speaker, I have never been, and I am not now, even after you have spoken to me for I have a speech impediment.

So, Moses had it all until he was forty as an Egyptian prince, then he fled for killing an Egyptian. Once a great orator, he now had a stutter; he became a shepherd then and only then was God able to use Moses as he had been broken, humbled, and gone through his own boot camp, led by God.

However, as Moses was now a humble man God said, "Now I am going to send you to Pharaoh to demand that he let you lead my people out of Egypt."

Jacob

What Jacob didn't realize was that he had just entered God's boot camp. He was in for a difficult twenty-year term under God's unwitting drillmaster, Laban. God would use these trying years to knock a lot of rough edges off Jacob.

Ultimately, yes, God would bless him. But part of the process involved breaking Jacob of his selfish ways.

In the Bible scripture:

> Jacob was alone; and a man wrestled with him until dawn. And the man saw that he could not win the match he struck Jacobs hip, and know it out of joint at the socket. Then the man said, "Let me go, for it is dawn." But Jacob panted, "I will not let you go until you bless me." What is your name the Man asked? Jacob was the reply. It isn't anymore the Man told him. It is Israel—one who has power with God. Because you have been strong with God, you shall prevail with men. (Gen. 32:24–28, TLB)

God promises to bless each person who trusts in Christ. Like Jacob, we say, "Sounds like a great program! Sure, I'll let you be my God if you'll bless me!" But we don't read the fine print that tells us that God's blessings always come through his discipline. To bless us and use us to bless others, God has to break us from our dependence on the flesh and shape us into the image of his Son, who learned obedience through the things he suffered.

As it says in the following Bible scripture:

> And even Jesus was God's son, he had to learn from experience what it was like

✝

to obey, when obeying meant suffering.
(Heb. 5:8, TLB)

So, God enrolls us in His boot camp. It's a tough program that lasts many years.

Joseph

The Story of Joseph (Here is a man whom went through God's boot camp) as described in the Bible in Genesis.

Joseph was born to Jacob late in Jacob's life and was his favorite, Joseph had eleven brothers and one sister. His brothers were really jealous of Joseph; they had thought about killing him. However, decided they did not want that on their conscious and then sold him as a slave for twenty pieces of silver.

He was sold to Portiphar, who brought Joseph back to have him work for him. In Genesis 39:2 (TLB) says:

> The Lord greatly blessed Joseph there in the home of his master, so everything he did succeeded.
>
> Portiphar saw that God was with him and put him in charge of his entire household. And God blessed Portiphar for this, however Portiphar's wife wanted Joseph to sleep with her, Joseph spurned her advances, so she told her husband that Joseph attacked her and so Portiphar had Joseph thrown in jail.

✝

In reading Genesis 39:21 (TLB), it says, "But the Lord was with Joseph there, too, and was kind to him by granting him favor with the Chief Jailer."

The chief jailer saw this and put Joseph in charge of the whole prison.

In Genesis 39:23 (TLB), "For the Lord was with him so that everything ran smoothly and well.

While in prison, the Pharaoh's Chief Baker and Wine taster had been put in jail and had some wild dreams, but they could not interpret what they meant."

In Genesis 40:8 (TLB), it says, "Interpreting dreams is God's business." Joseph replied, "Tell me what you saw." So, they tell him the dream and Joseph interprets it for them. And the Joseph tells them to please have some pity on him and mention him to the Pharaoh and ask him to let him out of jail.

So Pharaoh took the chief baker and the wine taster out of jail, and Joseph's interpretation of their dreams came true. The wine taster was out of jail promptly forgot about Joseph, never giving him a thought.

It was two years later when the pharaoh had a dream, called everyone together to try to help him figure it out. It was then that the wine taster told Pharaoh of what happened two years ago while in jail with the chief baker, and how there was a young Hebrew fellow there who told them what are dreams meant and everything happened just has he had interpreted them to be.

So, the pharaoh sent at once for Joseph (as described in Genesis 41:14–15) and told him that no one can tell me what these dreams means and that is why I have called for you.

✝

In Genesis 41:16 (TLB), it says, "I can't do it by myself, joseph replied, but God will tell you what it means!"

So, Joseph interpreted the pharaoh's dream and in Genesis 41:44, Pharaoh put Joseph in complete charge over all the land of Eygpt.

The dreams of the seven years of good crops and the seven years of famine came true.

During the famine years, Joseph's family ran out of food. His father, Jacob, sent Joseph's eleven brothers to Egypt to buy some grain. Joseph saw them, but they did not know it was Joseph. Joseph and put them through a series of tests, but in the end, told his brothers in Genesis 45:4–5 (TLB), "Come over here," he said, so they came closer. And he said again, "I am Joseph, your brother whom you sold into Egypt! But don't be angry with yourselves that you did this to me, for God did it! He sent me here ahead of you to preserve your lives."

Can you imagine that after all that Joseph had been through—sold into slavery, not sure if he would ever see if father again, his family again, then thrown into jail, to understanding and obeying God the whole time and then telling his brothers you did what God wanted you to do! And I still have tremendous love for you.

Could you imagine if God had told Joseph ahead of time what he was to go through and how by doing it his family would survive and be plentiful, I am not sure Joseph would have signed up for everything he went through.

I am joseph, your brother whom you sold
into Egypt! But don't be angry with your-

✝

selves that you did this to me, for God did it! He sent me here ahead of you to preserve your lives. (Gen. 45:4–5, TLB)

For Joseph succeeded in everything that he did because God was with him.

King David

Our God of Second Chances

Coach talks about the clearest picture that we have of God giving second chances is found in the story of King David. In Acts 13:22 (TLB), we read "God testified concerning him, I have found David son of Jesse, am man after my own heart: He will do everything I want him to do."

David was courageous and strong in battle, trusting God for protection. He loved God deeply and passionately.

David killed Goliath with a sling and a rock because he turned not to himself but to God for the victory.

He was constantly on the run from King Saul before he became king.

What mistakes did David make? *Big* ones, *huge* ones, He slept with one of his soldier's wife and got her pregnant. Then, to cover up his sin, he positioned the soldier in battle so that he would be surely killed.

Although he was a great military conqueror, David could not conquer himself. When confronted with his sin, he threw himself at the feet of God and asked for forgiveness.

One of the most appealing messages of Christianity is that we can be forgiven and that we serve a God of second chances.

> For David succeeded in everything that he did because God was with him. (1 Sam. 18:14, TLB)

Job

Job was a man of great character and wealth and he feared God. The Lord had blessed the work of Job's hands and his possessions increased throughout all the land.

Satan was allowed to test Job. He took Job's children and property. Then he attacks his health. However, during all this time, no matter how bad it got, he never bad-mouthed God. He thanked God every day.

As I started going through boot camp, with the loss of the prestigious jobs, money, and relationships I had, in the back of my mind, I wondered, *What are people thinking about me? Do they think I am a loser? Have they lost respect for me?* And after about a year of this, I finally surrendered to the fact the only one that matters who I think about me is that of my Heavenly Father.

Are you worried about what everyone else thinks and wondering how you can impress other people? I know that I sure did. I wanted to be liked and loved and I wanted to please everyone.

Joel Osteen wrote a daily scripture reminder which says, that we have to come to realize that when we come to the end of life, we are not going to stand before people and give an account of our lives. We are going to stand before the Almighty God. He is not going to say, "Why did you not do what so and so said to do? Why did you not fit their mold? Why did you not take their opinion?" No, he is going to ask. "Did you become whom I created you to be? Did you stay true to what I put in your heart?"

Osteen points out that Saul missed all God's blessings because he was insecure and afraid to disappoint somebody.

The passage in 1 Samuel 15:24 (TLB) says, "I have sinned," Saul finally admitted. "Yes, I have disobeyed your instructions and the command of the Lord, for I was afraid of the people and did what they demanded."

5

I Need to be a Fighter, Really?

Lonnie Berger, author of *Everyman a Warrior,* writes: "As Christian men we are constantly engaged in war. Whether we realize it or not, our life is the battlefield and Satan is our enemy. Most men have never been trained and equipped with the skills necessary to fight and end well."

Before I was in boot camp, I had never been trained and/or equipped with the skills necessary to fight the enemy or yet have it end well. In fact, I had no idea that what was causing my discomfort, tension within all my relationships, how I was feeling at work, even how I was feeling health wise was coming from the enemy, Satan himself.

Smith Wigglesworth wrote in his book *Greater Works:* "If by any means the enemy can come in and make you believe a lie, he will do so. It is in the closeness of the association and oneness with Christ that there is no fear, but perfect confidence all the time."

In the Bible scripture 2 Corinthians 11:14 (TLB) says, "Don't think that the devil is a big ugly monster he comes to you as an angel of the light. He comes at a time when you have done well and tells you about it He comes to make you feel you are somebody."

As I look back now at my getting fired from my job of almost twenty years, I believed everything the enemy said to me about all the successes I had and "the rules" did not apply to me.

This, too, is spiritual warfare as God is looking you to be humble and give all praise, glory, and honor to him.

The enemy has worked in people's mind and hearts, having people believe in their view of Christian men; that Christian men were not to make any mistakes. How could they call themselves Christians if they did make mistakes? It is as though they put Christian men on a pedestal, then wait until a mistake was made to knock the pedestal down so they could bring the Christian man down to their level and not have to get uncomfortable and get to know God.

I was one of those people for many years, and my thinking that a Christian man has to be perfect and be perfect all the time. However, there is only one that is perfect, and his name was Jesus Christ.

I saw a saying on a T-shirt that said,

- I am a Christian
- I am not perfect
- I make many mistakes
- However, God's grace for me is greater than any of the mistakes I have made

I have heard some men say that if I become Christian, I cannot live life to the fullest like I could if I was a non-Christian. I am here say, "Not true!" You are in spiritual warfare; the enemy tries to control your mind, your thinking, and does not want you to follow God.

As it states in the following Bible scripture of John 3:16 (TLB): "For God loved the world so much that he gave his only Son so that anyone who believes in him shall not perish but have eternal life."

Wow, how cool is that to have someone love us so much that he gave his only son for all of our sins. I have said it before, that it would be such a dishonor to God *not* to live life to the fullest as a Christian and not receive all the abundance God has to offer. We as Christians must have "audacious goals and aspirations" and as we achieve them, we must give *all praise, glory, and honor* to God for giving them to us.

When you say yes to Jesus and you commit your life to him that he is your Lord and Savior the enemy, Satan, will do anything to (steal, kill, and destroy) to take your relationship away. As a former non-believer, he left me alone, as I was not a threat to him. However, now as I am fully committed to God, he is constantly doing whatever he can to remove the relationship that I have with God.

It is a full-on spiritual warfare.

The tools that God gives us to fight spiritual warfare: Spiritual Warfare Toolkit

- Putting on the armor of God
- Praying
- Praying in the Holy Spirt

✝

- Praising God—Thank you, Father, for the training you are giving me to bring about your perfect will and plan for my life.
- Remember to rebuke the enemy—pronounce boldly, "In the name of Jesus, Satan be gone."

And finally, brothers, there is power to overcome everything, everything, everything in the world through *the name of Jesus*. Amen.

6

Salvation

The first step for me to becoming a son of God was to give up myself and turn my life over to Christ. Asking him for salvation which he is willing to give freely to all of us for free; we do not have to earn it.

A Christian's life is not that easy; salvation is free; however, it is costly to follow Christ. A Christians walk is a two-sided coin:

First, God saves us through Christ.
Second, we follow Christ in obedience to God.
The first part is God's, the seconds is ours.

Following Christ will cost us everything we are, as it says in the following Bible scriptures:

> Then Jesus said to the disciples, if anyone wants to be a follower of mine, let him deny himself and take up his cross and follow me. For anyone who keeps his life

for himself shall lose it and anyone who loses his life for me shall find it again. (Matt. 16:24–25, TLB)

Haven't you yet learned that your body is the home of the Holy Spirit, God gave you and that he lives within you your own body does not belong to you. (1 Cor. 6:19–20, TLB)

For salvation that come from Trusting Christ-which is what we preach-is already within easy reach of us, in fact it is as near as our own hearts and mouths. For if you tell others with your mouth that Jesus Christ is your Lord, and believe in your own heart that God has raised him from the dead you will be saved.

For it is believing in his heart that a man becomes right with God; and with his mouth he tells others of his faith, confirming his salvation. For the scriptures tells us that no one who believes in Christ will ever be disappointed.

Jew and Gentile are the same in this respect: they all have the same Lord who generously gives his riches to all those who ask him for them.

Anyone who calls upon the name of the Lord will be saved. (Rom. 10:8–13, TLB)

But didn't he earn his right to heaven by all the good things he did? No, for being saved is a gift, if a person could earn it by being good then is would not be, free-but it is. It is given to those who do not work for it. For God declares sinners to be good in his sight if they have faith in Christ to save them from God Wrath. (Rom. 4:4–5, TLB)

7

Faith

Faith is a crucial component in our *salvation,* in fact it is the only piece humans can contribute.

For those that are "of the world and in the world," what they see in the world is what they believe (seeing is believing). However, when you are "of the world and not in the world" and have salvation, faith is "believing is seeing." The Heavenly Father has abundant supernatural powers and that can change anything in the world in an instant.

The following Bible scriptures talk about having faith in God:

> For I am not ashamed of the Good News about Christ. It is God's powerful method of bringing all who believe it to heaven. This message was preached first to the Jews alone, but now everyone is invited to come to God in this same way. This Good News tells us that God makes us ready for heaven, makes us right in Gods sight

- when we put our faith and trust in Chris to save us. This is accomplished from start to finish by faith. As the scriptures says it. The man who finds life will find it through trusting God. (Rom. 1:16–17, TLB)

So God's blessings are given to us by faith, as a free gift. We are certain to get them whether or not we follow the Jewish customs if we have faith like Abrahams, for Abraham is the father of all of us when it comes to faith. (Rom. 4:16, TLB)

So it is that we are saved by faith in Christ and not by the good things we do. God treats us all the same. All whether Jews or Gentiles, are acquitted if they have faith. Well then if we are saved by faith, do this mean we no longer obey Gods laws? Just the opposite, in fact, only when we trust Jesus can we truly obey him. (Rom. 3:28, 30–31, TLB)

So now, since we have been made right in God's sight by faith in his promises we can have real peace with him because of what Jesus Christ our Lord has done for us. (Rom. 5:1–5, TLB)

For because of our faith, he has brought us into this place of highest privilege where we now stand, and we confidently and joyfully look forward to actually becoming all that God has had in his mind for us to be.

✝

We can rejoice, too, when we run into problems and trials, for we know that they are good for us—they help us learn to be patient.

And patience develops strength of character in us and helps us trust God more each time we use it until finally our hope and faith are strong and steady.

Then, when that happens, we are able to hold our heads high, no matter what happens and know that all is well, for we know how dearly God loves us and we feel this warm love everywhere within us because God has given us the Holy Spirit to fill our hearts with love.

Important Foundation of Christian Faith

Like the story of Jacob in the Bible, I, too, had a divine wrestling match with God. Until I had a very personal struggle with God, my faith was not cemented (Genesis 32:24–28).

Touch me just as he did overwhelming sense of peace.

8

Baptism

Most of us, after we were born, and while we're still quite young, our parents/guardians took us to get baptized. Being young, we did not have a choice. We were baptized Catholic, Protestant, Baptist, Lutheran, etc., what every religious church our parents/guardians were attending at the time or not.

As we get older and when we choose to accept Christ as our Lord and Savior, it is now our choice as to how we do that.

In the beginning of 2014, during my time with the Watchman, he asked me if I was baptized. In which I told him that, yes, my parents had taken me to their Lutheran church and I was baptized with the Lutheran religion. He then told me had I ever thought of getting baptized in water, through water immersion. I said no, I had not given it any thought. He said, "Just do me a favor and think about it."

So fast forward about nineteen months later, July 2015, and I had been working with the Reverend for about five months. He told me that he was going to be baptizing a person two weekends away in the Columbia River near where I was working. At the time, I thought nothing of it. Then it hit me what the Watchman had told me, "Think about just think about getting baptized in water." Baptism is a symbol. It is meant to show the world you love, trust, and have put your hope in Christ. A symbol of a new life as a Christian.

And as I thought more of it, I wanted to get baptized for myself, for my dedication to Christ, not because anyone else wanted me to do it, it was for me.

So, for my second step in becoming a son of God, I called the Reverend and asked him if I could be part of this baptism. He said it should not be a problem but wanted to call the other party involved to make sure it was okay. If it was not okay, then we would do it another time. However, the Reverend called me back and said it would be okay. So, on July 26, 2015, I was baptized by water immersion in the Columbia River.

As I continued my reading and research of the Bible, I found that every baptism in the Bible was by water immersion and the thought was that this was done to bury the old life and rise to walk in the new life. Baptism symbolizes the believer's total trust in and total reliance as well as their commitment to Christ.

"Going under the water was a burial of your old life, coming up out of the water is a resurrection of God raising you from the dead and he did Christ."

For sins power over us was broken when
we become Christians and we were bap-

tized to become a part of Jesus Christ, through his death the power of your sinful native was shattered.

Your old sin-loving native was buried with him by baptism when he died, and when God the Father with glorious power brought him back to life again, you were given his wonderful new life to enjoy. (Rom. 6:3–4, TLB)

Symbolic representation of the death, burial, and resurrection of Christ.

9

How Low Is the Bottom?

Two weeks after I was baptized, I moved out of the home I shared with the beautiful, loving, amazing woman who did what God called her to do, which was to let me go, so that God could have me fully.

I moved into my dad's house, which I lovingly called "the barracks" as I had a bedroom to sleep in, I had a part-time job at a retail home improvement store, I had to get state assistance to buy food to eat, continued to pay child support, and filed for bankruptcy.

I hit it, my bottom. I was broken to my core. I have heard before that God does not give you more than you can handle. There were times I would look up to heaven and say, "Really, God, I know that I have broad shoulders and I can carry a lot, but really."

In Smith Wigglesworth book *Greater Works*, he talks how to be useful to God: "He says you cannot talk about things you have not experienced, it seems to me God has a process of training us. You cannot take people to into the depths of God unless you have been broken yourself." I have been broken and broken and broken… praise God

As it says in Psalms 34:18, "The Lord is close to those who hearts are breaking." You must have the brokenness to get to the depths of God.

And I was really looking forward to knowing the depths of God because I was so broken.

God has a purpose for your pain, brothers, a reason for your struggles and a reward for your faithfulness.

10

Holy Spirit

And in the same way—by our faith—the Holy Spirit helps us with our daily problems and in our praying- For we don't even know what we should pray for, nor how to pray as we should; but the Holy Spirit prays for us with such feeling that it cannot be expressed into words. (Rom. 8:26, TLB)

Baptism of the Holy Spirit

As I continued my journey with the Reverend, I wanted more. I wanted to go deeper in my relationship with the Lord. So in March of 2016, for my third step in becoming a son of God, I asked the Reverend to baptize me with the Holy Spirit on my birthday, which is in June, and he agreed.

The Reverend suggested that I get Smith Wigglesworth book *Greater Works* as it would be the guide along with the

Bible in which he would use to teach me about the Holy Spirit, the power it gives. So, I went out and purchased the book by Smith Wigglesworth and began to read and to understand all about the Holy Spirit. If I had a question about what I was reading, I would text or call the Reverend and we would discuss and have fellowship at length about the wonderfulness of having the Holy Spirit live inside me.

So, in June of 2016, on my birthday, the Reverend and I went to a park in the town in which we lived. And on that sunny day in nature, the Reverend baptized me in the Holy Spirit.

The following Bible scripture states the following:

> Seven weeks had gone by since Jesus's death and resurrection and the day of Pentecost had now arrived. As the believers met that day.
>
> Suddenly there was a sound like the roaring of a mighty windstorm in the skies about them and it filled the house where they were meeting.
>
> Then, what looked like flames or tongues of fire appeared and settled on their heads
>
> And everyone present was filled with the Holy Spirit and began to speak in a language they did not know for the Holy Spirit gave them this ability. (Acts 2:1–4, TLB)

✝

Twenty minutes after I was baptized, I began to pray in the Holy Spirit language for almost an hour straight, and then the Holy Spirit spoke to me and said, "I am within you now and forever more."

Smith Wigglesworth wrote in *Greater Works*, "When the Holy Spirit gets ahold of a person, he is a new man entirely, his whole being becomes saturated with divine power."

After the Holy Spirit comes upon you, you will have power, God will mightily move within your life, the Holy Spirit will overshadow you, inwardly moving you until you know there is a divine plan different from anything you have had in your life before.

If you are ready to receive this life, it is amazing how it will quicken your mortal body every time you touch this life.

"It is divine life, it is the life of a son of God." (Rom. 8:11, TLB)

You will go from being ordinary to extraordinary as you have an extraordinary God whom gives you revelation.

Remember, brothers, pray all the time, ask God for anything in line with the Holy Spirit's wishes. Plead with him, reminding him of your needs, and keep praying earnestly for all Christians everywhere.

And finally, brothers, there is power to overcome everything, everything, everything in the world through the name of Jesus.

As it is said in the following Bible scripture:

For all who are led by the Spirit of God are sons of God

And so, we should not be like cringing, fearful slaves, but we should behave like Gods very own children, adopted in the bosom of his family and calling him Father, Father

For his Holy Spirit speaks to us deep in our hearts and tells us that we are really Gods children.

And since we are his children, we will share his treasures—for all God gives to his Son Jesus is now ours too. But if we are to share his glory, we must share is suffering.

Yet suffer now is nothing compared to the glory he will give us later. (Rom. 8:14–18, TLB)

My brothers, yes, the suffering can be tough, and it most likely will be. However, if you want to be great in anything, you must put in the time, train, be coached to be the greatest that you can be. Whether it be studying for an exam, playing football, basketball, baseball, soccer, driving a stockcar in the Nascar Cup Series or a ten-thousand-horsepower Dragster in the NHRA Melloyellow series, the greatest elite athletes, business executives, astronauts, put in the extra work, in the weight room, watch film of your opponent; whatever it takes to be the best, whether it be taking away time from your family, the other things that you like to do, to be the best you can be. So, taking the time, the suffering to become a son of God.

The following Bible scriptures talk about a life living with the Holy Spirit inside you:

> Not only so, but we also glory in our suffering, because we know that suffering produces perseverance; perseverance, character; and character, hope. And hope does not put us to shame, because Gods love has been poured out into our hearts through the Holy Spirit, whom has been given to us. (Rom. 5:3–5, TLB)
>
> I am the Way—yes and the Truth and Life. No one can get to the Father except by means of me. (Jn 14:16, TLB)
>
> If we are live now by the Holy Spirits power, let us follow the Holy Spirits leading in every part of our lives. Then we won't need to look for honors and popularity, which lead to jealousy and hard feelings. (Gal. 5:25–26, TLB)
>
> Those who let themselves be controlled by their lower natures live only to please themselves but those who follow after the Holy Spirit find themselves doing those things that please God, following after the Holy Spirit leads to life and peace, but following after the old nature leads to death. (Rom. 8:5–6, TLB)

✝

Says that in on these meeting Jesus told the disciples not to leave Jerusalem until the Holy Spirit comes down upon them in fulfilment of the Father's promises. John baptized you with water, he reminded them, but you will be baptized with the Holy Spirit in just a few days. (Acts 1:4–5, TLB)

Jesus tells them when the Holy Spirit has come upon you, you will receive power to testify about me with Great effect. (Acts 1:8, TLB)

When the council saw the boldness of Peter and John and could see that they were obviously uneducated non-professionals, there were amazed and realized what being with Jesus had done for them. (Acts 4:13, TLB)

✝

11

Keeping Your Eyes on the Prize

As I have progressed with my journey with the Lord, there have been times when I took back control, thinking I was the one doing all the wonderful things in my life, and during those times that I was not putting God first. I would think about employment, money, relationships, at which point the enemy would find his way in and steal my joy and my happiness. I would worry about all this that I could not control, but God had a handle on it.

You can't fail if God is in it: the Bible portrays only two individuals walking on water; Jesus and Peter as it is written in Matthew 14:27–31. This is a great story of having the courage to following the Lord's calling and the humility to turn to him when the going gets tough. Peter had the guts to step out of the boat, but like many of us when the wind and waves kicked up (distractions or current reality (seeing is believing), he took his eyes of Jesus; he panicked and began to sink. However, when he called out to the Lord, he was saved.

But Jesus spoke to them, reassuring them "Don't be afraid," he said.

Then Peter called to him: "Sir, if it is really you tell me to come over to you, walking on the water."

"All right," the Lord said, "Come along."

So, Peter went over the side of the boat and walked on water toward Jesus. But when he looked at the high waves, he was terrified and began to sink. "Save me, Lord," he shouted

Instantly, Jesus reached out his hand and rescued him. "O, man, of little faith," Jesus said. "Why did you doubt me?" (Matt. 14:27–31, TLB)

What an amazing story here an ordinary, uneducated man walked on water as he believed and kept his eyes on Jesus.

However as soon as he looked at the situation around him "high waves and gusts of wind he began to sink and when he cried out "Jesus" immediately he gave him his hand.

For me, my situation around me was lack of employment, relationship, and financial status, the enemy came in and stole my joy, so I called Jesus and he gave me his hand.

✝

12

Your Best Investment Ever

In Lonnie Berger's *Every Man a Warrior* book, he wrote the following statement:

Men, we are all going to die! I find every man, Christian or not, deep down on the inside wonders, *When I die, will I have accomplished anything? Will my life have a made a difference?*

Make sure your life counts. The best investment you will ever make is that of becoming a son of God. For yourself, for your family, and for all your descendants. You will be leaving a lasting legacy.

The road to becoming a son of God will not be an easy one. It will be filled with potholes, curves, twists, trials, and tribulations. The enemy, Satan, will be hiding, waiting for an opportunity to come and steal your joy, happiness.

Remember, when you come to accept Christ, and start your relationship with him, the battle is on.

And that Jesus is never late (he usually does not come on our time), and he wants you to be of the world, but not in it.

The following Bible scripture sums this investment up the best:

> Don't store up treasures here on earth where they can erode away or be stolen. Store them in heaven where they will never lose their value and are safe from thieves. If your profits are in heaven your heart will be there also. (Matt. 6:19–21, TLB)

13

Same Power

When you are filled with the Holy Spirit, you have the same power as Jesus, as the disciples. You have the power to rebuke the evil spirits; you have the power to heal. You are now a son of God.

Remember, brothers, there is such power to overcome everything, everything, everything in the world through the name of Jesus. Rebuking the enemy, healing the sick, and pronouncing boldly "In the name of Jesus!"

Jeremy Camp sings about this with his song "Same Power"

I can see
Waters raging at my feet
I can feel
The breath of those surrounding me
I can hear
The sound of nations rising up
We will not be overtaken

We will not be overcome
I can walk
Down this dark and painful road
I can face
Every fear of the unknown
I can hear
All God's children singing out
We will not be overtaken
We will not be overcome
The same power that rose Jesus from the grave
The same power that commands the dead to wake
Lives in us, lives in us
The same power that moves mountains when He
speaks
The same power that can calm a raging sea
Lives in us, lives in us
He lives in us, lives in us
We have hope
That His promises are true
In His strength
There is nothing we can't do
Yes, we know
There are greater things in store
We will...
The same power that rose Jesus from the grave
The same power that commands the dead to wake
Lives in us, lives in us
The same power that moves mountains when He
speaks
The same power that can calm a raging sea

Lives in us, lives in us
He lives in us, lives in us
Greater is He that is living in me
He's conquered our enemy
No power of darkness
No weapon prevails
We stand here in victory
Oh
Greater is He that is living in me
He's conquered our enemy
Oh
No power of darkness
No weapon prevails
We stand here in victory
Oh, in victory
Yeah
The same power that rose Jesus from the grave
The same power that commands the dead to wake
Lives in us, lives in us
The same power that moves mountains when He
speaks
The same power that can calm a raging sea
Lives in us, lives in us
He lives in us, lives in us
He lives in us

✝

14

Wrap Up

I read the following during my research for this book: "The God who created me and loves me, he is my primary audience, everything else will fall into line—professionally and personally. Most important, I'll continue to grow spiritually."

Remember the Joel Osteen daily scripture reminder which says that we have to come to realize that when we come to the end of life, we are not going to stand before people and give an account of our lives. We are going to stand before the Almighty God, he is not going to say "Why did you not do what so and so said to do? Why did you not fit their mold? Why did you not take their opinion?" No, he is going to ask, "Did you become whom I created you to be? Did you stay true to what I put in your heart?"

God has a purpose for your pain, a reason for your struggles and a reward for your faithfulness.

So, I have been in this God-led spiritual boot camp for close to three years. I have lost a relationship in which I had my heart wide open with unconditional and unguarded love for the first time in my life. I have gone through feelings of abandonment and rejection. I have had to live in a motor home, live with my dad; I had to file for bankruptcy and I have had to file and receive state assistance for food. I am underemployed at the moment; however, God has told me that as I am going through boot camp, that he will provide all that I need, not what I want, but what I need. I can say that he has not failed me.

As I look at where I am today, my life before me was filled with insecurities, lying, and manipulation, thinking that I was not worthy of what life had to offer. I was not leading my life and my relationships, my own house, good car; that I was not the head of the house, the man God wanted me to be.

I am so grateful and blessed for God in my life and molding me into the man he wants me to be. I have been broken down to the core. I feel like a phoenix that has been burned to ashes and now is being reborn.

I am creating the life I want with God leading.

Let me leave you with a couple of thoughts:

- *Recognize and submit to God's hand in the daily events of your life.* Things don't just happen to you. You haven't had a spell of bad luck. God arranges your circumstances to shape you into the image of Jesus Christ.
- *Don't run from the difficult people in your life until God gives you the okay.* If you're married to the difficult person, God isn't giving the okay! We all tend to run from the difficult people God puts in our

lives to shape us. If you've got a difficult person in your life, rather than complaining about him/her and running from him/her, ask yourself what God is trying to teach you about yourself through this person.

- *Plan to persevere over the long haul.* Christianity isn't a one-hundred-yard dash; it's a marathon. In today's society, a lot of people want instant answers to their problems, and when they don't get them, they bail out and go looking for some other solution. Brothers, as Winston Churchill once said, "Never, never, never give up!"

- *Thank God for the gracious blessings he bestows.* Sure, the discipline hurts, but God only does it because He loves us as a father loves his children. With the discipline, He weaves in ample doses of grace, so that we can enjoy even the hard times.

- *Read the Bible and pray consistently.*

As much as the disciple Peter messed up, Jesus still loved him very much and he was one of his favorites.

- Ecclesiastes 7:20 (TLB) says, "And there is not a single man in all the earth who is always good and never sins.
- I am a Christian
- I am not perfect
- I mess up
- But God's grace is bigger than my sins.

✝

So, this has been my journey so far and has brought me to this point in my life. Don't take my word for it, go do you own research, your own testing, the world is your laboratory.

Much Love,
Brian

If you want to accept Jesus as your Savior pray the following:

God, I believe that Jesus died on the cross for my sins. Please forgive me for all my sins. Jesus, I ask you to be my Lord and Savior. God, I now take you as my Father. Amen.

If you prayed this prayer, I believe you are now born again.

Addendum

Men of God in your relationship with your wife/girlfriend

- Lead her like Abraham
- Fight for her love like Jacob
- Care for her like Boaz
- Love her like Christ.

Remember as a son of God

- Be strong but not rude
- Be kind but not weak
- Be humble but not timid
- Be bold but not arrogant

Brian's steps for becoming a son of God

1. Accept the Lord as your Savior
2. Baptism in the water
3. Baptism of the Holy Spirit

About the Author

 Just like Peter said to Cornelius in Acts 10:26, "I am too just a man like you." I, too, say to you I am just a man like you. I am a man that has gotten up one more times than I have been knocked down, and I am here to tell you that I have been knocked down many many times. For over fifty years, I tried to fill up the inside from the material world (money, career, cars, relationships) on the outside, and now my inside is filled up with my Heavenly Father, the Lord Jesus, and the Holy Spirit and I do not envy any man. All praise, glory, and honor goes to God. I am writing books with the sole purpose of bringing men to Christ.

✝

To Caleb aka MC Numan,

Keep on rappin.

May God continue to bless you and your family,

Brian

CPSIA information can be obtained
at www.ICGtesting.com
Printed in the USA
FFHW021016271118
49659552-54038FF

9 781643 491868